A Complete Kid's Guide to Fossils

Discover how different types of fossils are formed, what they reveal about the past, and where to find them

By A. Cox

DEDICATION:

This book is dedicated to my sister. Because of her childhood dream of becoming a paleontologist, I was able to dig into the amazing world of fossils. Thank you for all of the memories hunting for fossils in the midwest. I'll always remember the time we found that trilobite.

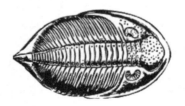

Dear Reader,
Thank you so much for reading my book! As a special thank you, scan the QR code below to get your free Nature Detective's Handbook, a fun activity book that includes over 50 pages of activities for your child to explore more of the outdoors! Designed specifically for the US state parks!

TABLE OF CONTENT

INTRODUCTION

Hello there, fellow fossil fanatic!

Have you ever thought about what is hidden underground? Sure, there are holes that animals live in and caves with amazing rock formations in them, but what about other secrets hidden in the dirt? Imagine if you could hold a physical piece of the past. It could be something like the tooth or claw from a shark or T-Rex or an insect trapped in a pearl of amber. How cool would that be? These incredible things are both different types of fossils and they can give us a snapshot into what the past was like a long time ago...but only if you know where to look for them and how to understand them.

But how are fossils formed? Fossils are formed in different ways and different conditions. One example is a plant or animal that died and then buried under something else, like mud, sand, or ash from a volcano. Then, millions and millions of years pass. Each year, more layers of dirt or mud are piled on top, increasing the pressure on the dead plant or animal. Similar to how coal under pressure becomes a diamond, these animals or plants turn into stone under all of those layers. This process is called 'fossilization' and it is nature's way of making sure the plants and animals of past eras are never forgotten.

But how are fossils formed? Fossils are formed in different ways and different conditions. One example is a plant or animal that died and then buried under something else, like mud, sand, or ash from a volcano. Then, millions and millions of years pass. Each year, more layers of dirt or mud are piled on top, increasing the pressure on the dead plant or animal.

Similar to how coal under pressure becomes a diamond, these animals o
plants turn into stone under all of those layers. This process is called
'fossilization' and it is nature's way of making sure the plants and animals o
past eras are never forgotten.

Fossils are really cool…but that's not all they are. They are like a physical

piece of the earth's origin
story. Fossils show us a lot o
things that were around way
before humans appeared
There are fossils from animal
and plants on land, in the

oceans, and even animals that fly! One interesting thing that fossils can teach
us about the history of the earth is how the oceans and land changed ove
time. Fossils can show us how climate and the weather changed over time o
even give us clues about why dinosaurs and other animals disappeared.

So how can you get your hands on some fossils of your own? Fossil
can be found anywhere in the world, including mountains, in the sea
deserts, on the beach, or even in your local park.[1] There have been famou
fossil discoveries all over the world. The coolest part of all of this is that yo
don't have to be specially trained or have fancy equipment to find fossils.

Fossils can be found all around us but only by people who have patience,
sense of adventure, and a sharp eye.

In this book, you'll take a journey through time….or is it a journe
through dirt? Anyway, you'll explore how different kinds of fossils are mac
and what they can tell us about earth's history. You'll also learn where yo
can find these different fossils too! Also at the end of the book is a full list o

references that were used to find some extra information. Each of the links also has some pretty great photos of the fossils described so be sure to ask your parents if you can look at these links to see some more pictures of fossils.

So, grab your magnifying glass and let's start digging into the past!

It is even possible to find fossils in your local park!

Chapter 1:

❖

DISCOVERING THE GIANTS OF THE PAST

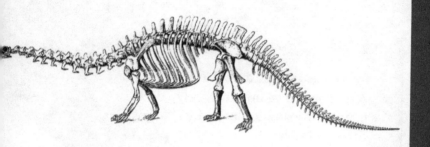

In this chapter, we will focus on the most famous type of fossils: animal fossils. We will learn all about animal fossils, including how they are made, the different types of fossils, where the dinosaurs lived and more. We will also learn about what fossils tell us about the anatomy of prehistoric animals, why they went extinct, and how dinosaurs adapted to their environment over time.

1.1 INTRO TO FOSSILS

Even though there are multiple ways that fossils are formed, the most common way that fossils are formed is through a process called 'permineralization.' Bone, teeth, and shell fossils are mostly this form of fossil. Permineralization happens when minerals in groundwater – water that moves through the ground – get stuck inside of the cells of dead animals. These dissolved minerals 'get organized' and become crystals which eventually, become rock. So how does the groundwater flow through the animal cells?

How are fossils formed?

A dinosaur dies and the body is not eaten immediately by other animals

Well, long before the ground water starts to move through the dead dinosaur's cells, the dinosaur is covered with many layers of dirt–also called 'sediment.' The first few layers of sediment cover the body of the dead animal quickly; this is how the dinosaur's body is mostly preserved. After the dinosaur has been covered, more and more layers of sediment and volcanic ash piles on top of it. The layers that are covering the dinosaur body harden and become rock, keeping the body safe inside.[2]

Now, even though the body is buried somewhat quickly, there will still be some of the body missing by the time it is covered. This could be because some scavengers ate part of it (like vultures or crabs) or the soft parts of the body decomposed naturally before it was buried.[3] That's why some fossils have only part of the bones, while others are fully formed and even others have soft tissue, like feathers!

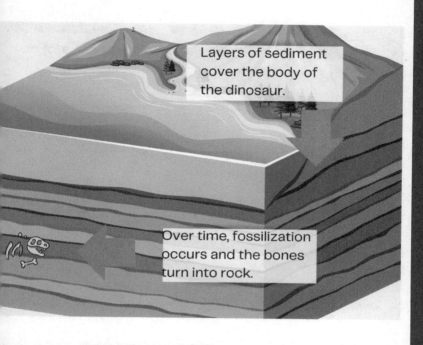

Layers of sediment cover the body of the dinosaur.

Over time, fossilization occurs and the bones turn into rock.

1.2 WHAT FOSSILS REVEAL

Even though dinosaurs have been dead for a really long time, paleontologists (the people who study fossils), have a lot of really specialized tools that they can use to examine the fossils they find and learn from them. First, they look at the way that the bones were found in the rock. The shape that the bones were found in can give clues about how the bones fit together when the dinosaur was alive. Seeing the bones that are next to each other can often show where the dinosaur had a joint (like a knee or elbow) and this shows how the dinosaur moved.[4] Sometimes, the bones or joints they find in the rocks are very similar to animals that are still around today. The paleontologists can compare the dinosaur to the animal that is still living and see how the dinosaur may have lived or moved.

Paleontologists use a lot of different tools to study fossils.

Paleontologists can also learn a lot from looking at other thing besides bones. Teeth, for example, are often fossilized with the bones of th dinosaur. If a dinosaur skeleton has been found that has lots of sharp point teeth, then the scientists can guess that this dinosaur was a predator and a other animals or dinosaurs. On the other hand, if the dinosaur skeleton ha lots of flat teeth, it probably ate a lot of plants. Recently, scientists have als been able to use microscopes to study scratches in the teeth that they fin This allows them to make guesses about what specific plants or animals th dinosaurs ate.[4]

Some fossils can even tell scientists more about how the dinosa looked when it was alive. For example, fossils of dinosaurs with scales an feathers have been found! That shows us that there is a connection betwee dinosaurs and modern day birds.[4] It can be hard to believe when you look a chicken or a flamingo but it is true! Dinosaurs are related to birds.

Some fossils have been found with feathers on them, showing a connection between dinosaurs and modern birds

And since birds nowadays can be studied and scientists know that dinosaurs are related to birds, many scientists believe that fossils show that some dinosaurs have similar social behavior to those of birds. For example, many modern-day birds have flashy feathers around the head that are used to attract a mate. Some dinosaur fossils have frills around the head that seem too fragile for defending themselves against an attack. The paleontologists suspect that this frill may be used to attract a mate, just like birds who have flashy feathers.[5] However, since there are no real living dinosaurs around, it impossible to know for sure how they behaved!

While we can't say for sure which behaviors from dinosaurs' modern relatives existed in the past, we can trace the connection between birds and dinosaurs through fossils. Birds originally evolved from a group of dinosaurs called 'theropods.'[6] This group of dinosaurs contained many types of dinosaurs, including the T. Rex and the spinosaurus, and is a group of dinosaurs that all have hollow bones and three toes on their feed (just like birds!).[7] According to the fossil record, the oldest bird fossils are around 150 million years old and they had some things that are similar to modern birds but also some different things. These bird fossils had feathers, of course, but also the mouths of the birds had sharp teeth![6]

Scientists discovered that birds evolved from theropods...Another theropod you may know? The T. Rex!

This seems like a lot of information to get from a few dusty old bones but actually we've only just scratched the surface of what can still be learned from dinosaur fossils. There's still more that fossils can tell us! Now scientists are looking deeper into what the fossils can tell us about how the animals and dinosaurs of the past were affected by different types of climate changes.[8]

1.3 CHECK YOUR KNOWLEDGE!

Check how much you remember from this chapter by choosing the correct answer to each of the following questions!

What is the most common way that fossils are formed?

a. Burning
b. Freezing
c. Permineralization
d. Decomposition

How do minerals get into the dead animals' cells during permineralization?

a. Animals swallow the minerals.
b. Minerals in the ground water flow into the cells.
c. Minerals form on the outside of the animal's body.
d. Animals absorb the minerals from the soil.

What helps protect the dinosaur's body as it gets buried?

a. Scavengers
b. Layers of sediment
c. Decomposition
d. Leaves

What do paleontologists look at to learn about how dinosaurs moved?

a. The shape of the bones
b. The color of the bones
c. The size of the bones
d. The weight of the bones

5. *What connection do fossils show between dinosaurs and modern birds?*

    a. Some dinosaurs had flat teeth like birds.

    b. Some dinosaurs had feathers and hollow bones like birds.

    c. Some dinosaurs had sharp claws like birds.

    d. Some dinosaurs had wings like birds.

Chapter 2:

---✤---

AMBER FOSSILS:

PRESERVING LIFE IN GOLDEN DROPS

In this chapter, we will focus on a different type of fossil. This fossil – called amber – is actually a stone that is made from the resin of a prehistoric tree. We'll learn all about amber, including how amber is created, how amber is different from other fossils, and what things we can learn about the prehistoric world from amber. Later in the book, in Chapter 6, we'll even find out where you can find amber on your own!

2.1 HOW AMBER FOSSILS FORM

Amber is formed when the resin from a tree leaks out of the tree. This resin is very sticky and doesn't dissolve in water; actually, it gets really hard when it touches air. When the tree is alive, the resin acts as a way for the tree to heal from some injury, like when humans get a cut and then there is a scab afterwards. When the tree gets damaged in some way – for example, if a branch breaks off or a crack in the trunk forms – resin seeps out of the damaged area and hardens over it creating a shield against other things that might damage the tree.[14]

Prehistoric tree resin gets buried under layers of sediment and becomes amber

Because the resin is so sticky, lots of other plants or insects may ge stuck in the resin. When they get stuck, they can't get out and eventually, a more resin leaks out of the tree, the plants or animals get fully stuck inside of the resin. Eventually, these trees die and fall down and are then buried under layers of sediment.Other times, the resin may fall off of the tree into som water or a swamp. If it falls into water, the movement of the water and seabed may cover the resin. In both cases, the resin is under pressure for long time. Scientists say that all amber is at least 40,000 years old! [14]

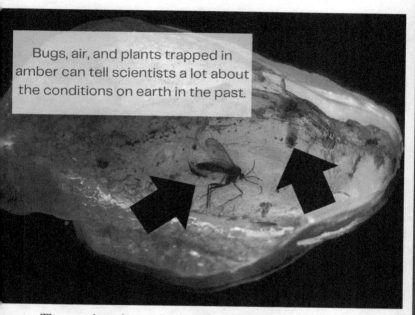

Bugs, air, and plants trapped in amber can tell scientists a lot about the conditions on earth in the past.

These amber pieces with the bugs and plants still inside have been studied by scientists for over two hundred years. Because the amber hardens over the fragile animals and plants, it protects everything inside of it, providing scientists with a very clear picture of how some bugs and plants looked in the past. This is important because with other fossilization methods, insects are easily squashed so they aren't around long enough to really fossilize well.[14]

So what are paleontologists looking for when they find amber? Scientists can use the things trapped in amber to create a snapshot of what the world was like when the amber first leaked out of the tree as resin.The creatures, the plants and plant parts (like leaves, seeds, and pollen), and even the bubbles of air or water trapped inside the amber give scientists detailed information about what the world was like at the creation of that amber.

For example, in the world's most famous amber deposit – the Baltic Sea – scientists have identified and studied over 3,500 different types of arthropods.[14] Arthropods are the type of animals that include insects, spiders, centipedes, and even crabs.[15] In the second largest amber deposit, found in the Dominican Republic in the Caribbean Sea, over 1000 different species of arthropods have been found. Fish and other vertebrates have also been found in amber here, though rarely.[14]

The Baltic Sea has the world's richest deposit of amber

These two locations, the Baltic Deposit and the Dominican Deposit, can tell us about two different specific times in the past because the amber found at each of these deposits are different ages. The amber found in the Baltic region is estimated to be about 34 to 38 million years old while the Dominican amber is said to be around 15 to 20 million years old.[14] That's how scientists can learn about a specific time using amber. They know the age of the amber and can compare the different animals and plants they found that are also estimated to be the same age.

But how do scientists figure out the age of the amber fossils? Well, because amber comes from trees, which are considered organic material, they can use carbon dating. Carbon dating is a little complicated but basically, scientists use an element called Carbon to help measure how old something is. 'Normal' carbon has a weight of 12 and an 'irregular' weight of 14. All living things take in the carbon 14 type (C-14) while they are alive and then the C-14 starts to disappear after the living thing dies. Scientists know the speed that C-14 disappears. By measuring how much C-14 is left in the dead thing's tissue, they know how long the thing has been dead.

This method for checking the age of organic material is accurate for things that died up to 60,000 years ago.[16] Some of the amber that has been collected can be dated using the carbon dating method however, many of the amber deposits around the world are much older than 60,000 years. If the amber is suspected of being older than this, the scientists can use a similar method but with a different element that disappears at a slower speed than C-14. They can also tell how old the amber is based on the age of the rocks and dirt around the amber, but this method doesn't work if the amber is found on the coastline or in a river.

2.2 WHAT AMBER FOSSILS REVEAL

Paleoecology – the study of ecosystems from prehistoric times – has benefited greatly from studying amber with animals or plants stuck inside.[19] As mentioned before, studying the insects and other things trapped in amber – called inclusions – can help scientists build a snapshot of what the world looked like in ancient times. The insects and plants are so well-preserved that scientists are able to use them to connect various links between different parts of ancient ecosystems.[17] For example, sometimes two insects were trapped together, like in a famous amber find from Myanmar. In this amber, both a spider and a wasp were trapped ... and the spider was eating the wasp![18] Amber has trapped other sorts of interactions between animal species and from these, scientists are able to study the eating or behavioral habits of arthropods trapped in amber.

The things that get stuck in the sticky resin are called 'inclusions'

Because amber protects squishy creatures in a hard shell, the scientis are able to see things that they aren't able to with other fossil types.F example, while rock fossils occasionally have imprints of feathers, amber able to preserve the actual strands from the feather. Eleven different amb pieces in Canada have been found with feathers that dated as far back as million years old.[18] It is easy to see how amber gives such great insight to t prehistory world.

Another example of how amber preserves the ecology of the past in a recent discovery made in Myanmar, where another major amber depo is located. This amber trapped a termite from 100 million years ago. T termite was trapped in amber after its stomach area had been ripped ope Out of this termite's open stomach flowed a type of single-celled animals alled protozoans. Similar protozoans help modern-day termites digest wood that they've eaten. So thanks to this amber, scientists were able to discover that, as far back as 100 million years ago, termites were helped by protozoans.[20] Other things that scientists can learn about plants from amber the approximate size of prehistoric trees.

While amber has helped scientists learn about the ancient past for over two hundred years, amber has been around in human history for much longer. Amber has been around in human history for over 2000 years! The first written mention of amber was in the 4th century BCE.[21] The most common use of amber in the early human history years was as jewelry.In ct, it has been used in jewelry as far back as 13000 years ago![21] Amber was so used in ancient civilizations as natural medicines but the Food and Drug ssociation in the US recommends against using amber for medicinal urposes.[21] Finally, the lovely pine smell that amber gives off makes it a popular choice for perfume ingredients in several cultures around the world, including ancient China.[21]

2.3 CHECK YOUR KNOWLEDGE!

Check how much you remember from this chapter by choosing th correct answer to each of the following questions!

1. *What does amber come from?*

    a. Rocks
    b. Dinosaur bones
    c. Tree sap
    d. Seashells

2. *What can get stuck in the sticky tree sap as it hardens into amber?*

    a. Air
    b. Leaves and plants
    c. Feathers
    d. All of the above

3. *How do scientists figure out how old amber is?*

    a. They ask the person who found it
    b. They count the layers of the amber
    c. They use a special tool to measure the age
    d. They use carbon dating

4. *What is one advantage of amber fossils compared to other types of fossil.*

    a. Amber fossils are more colorful
    b. Amber fossils are bigger
    c. Amber fossils are better preserved
    d. Amber fossils are easier to find

5. *What can scientists learn about ancient ecosystems by studying the things trapped in amber?*

   a. Rocks
   b. Dinosaur bones
   c. Tree sap
   d. Seashells

Chapter 3:

AQUATIC CREATURE FOSSILS
UNVEILING THE SECRETS OF ANCIENT AQUATIC CREATURES

In this chapter, we are going to learn about how prehistoric aquatic creatures turned into fossils. Fossils of aquatic animals are formed in a similar way to how fossils of land creature fossils are formed but with some differences. We'll also discover the three main types of aquatic fossils you may find: ammonites, trilobites, and vertebrates–animals with backbones. So let's dive in!

3.1 HOW SEA CREATURE FOSSILS FORM

Earlier in the book, we learned how fossils on land were created. D
you remember how they form? Let's have a quick review before moving or
First, the animal or dinosaur dies and then their body is covered by layer
and layers of sediment. These layers and the bones harden into rock and th
remaining parts of the body are what create the fossils. With aquati
creatures, fossils are formed a little differently.

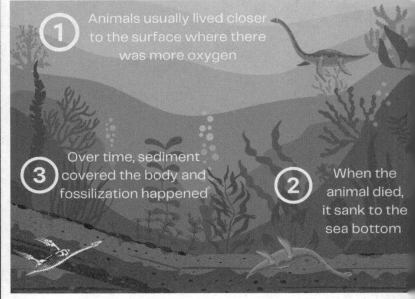

First, let's think about the water in lakes, rivers, and oceans. T
water near the surface is very oxygen-rich. This means there is a lot
oxygen available to the animals that live there. On the flip side, the wat
near the bottom of the lake, river, or ocean is oxygen-poor so fewer anim;
can live there.[22] Also, the deeper the water is, the more pressure there is
the bottom–called the sediment. Imagine how the water looks from surf;
to the seabed: near the surface, there are many different types of fish t
deeper down, there are fewer types of creatures.

Eventually, all of these creatures die and sink all the way down to the bottom, all piling on top of each other.[22]   Mud settles on top of these creatures. Over time, more creatures and more mud settle to the bottom of the water. The immense pressure of the water and of the creatures and mud settling on top of the layers of other creatures eventually crushes the layers into limestone.[23] Most of the time, these animal shells and bones are squished into dust but not always. The shells and bones that remain whole are the fossils that scientists use to study ancient aquatic life.[24] Because there were fewer things in the water that would eat the animal after it died and also because the sediment immediately began to cover the animal's body, it was far more likely that an aquatic animal became a fossil than a land animal. So what aquatic fossils are you likely to find?

Ammonites and brachiopods are the most common type of fossil you may find because of the hard shell. Ammonites look similar to a

Brachiopod Fossil

Ammonite Fossil

modern-day nautilus but lived around the time that the dinosaurs lived. They also died in the extinction event that killed the dinosaurs 65 million years ago.[25] Brachiopods are much older and look like clams. Of course, clams still exist today but 400 million years ago, there were many more species than there are today![25]

Another couple of invertebrate fossils that you might be able to find are trilobite and coral fossils. These are among the oldest fossils that have ever been found! Trilobites are like the great-great-great-great-grandparents of modern-day crabs and other crustaceans. These animals are over 521 million years old![26] Trilobites are easy to recognize because of their three-part body. It looks a bit like if you hold three fingers together. Coral has been around in the earth's oceans since around 500 million years ago.[27] Coral that grow in colonies are the easiest fossil types to recognise because they are large and often look like repeated patterns in rocks.Sometimes, coral fossils even look like branches of a tree.[28]

Of course, there are also fish and other vertebrate fossils that you might find too. Depending on where you go, it is possible to find a very wide variety of fish fossils!

Trilobite Fossils

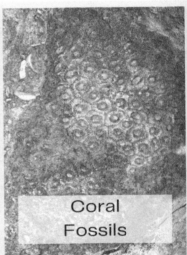
Coral Fossils

For example, in Fossil Butte (USA), you can find fish, stingrays, paddlefish and so many other types of fossils.[29] Finding a fish or a stingray can be an amazing way to spend a day outdoors but what do these aquatic fossils tell us about ancient and modern marine ecosystems?

3.2 WHAT AQUATIC FOSSILS REVEAL

Just like looking at fossils of land animals or looking at the inclusions in amber can tell us a lot about the environment on land at a specific point in the past, the same is true for aquatic fossils. In fact, the diversity of this type f fossil gives a lot of insight to other things too, not just how the ancient eas and lakes were in the past.One of the things that scientists look at when ney study fossils is how ancient animals evolved. For example, trilobites first ppeared on the fossil record around 521 million years ago but they didn't isappear from the fossil record until 251 million years ago.[30] The first ilobites found look very different to the trilobites found in the strata dated 51 million years old.Scientists look at the changes and can learn a lot about ow the environment changed for trilobites (and the other animals living at ne same time).

cientists can also look at the fossil record and see when specific animals first ame into the fossil record and if they evolved so much over time that they volved into their modern counterpart. It is even possible to find animals on ne fossil record from millions of years ago that are still around almost xactly the same today! For example, the earliest fossil of a frill shark – a pecies of shark that lives in some of the deepest waters of the ocean – was und to be 80 million years old. Modern frill sharks still look almost entical to the fossil frill shark.[31] That's pretty amazing to think about! ther examples of aquatic animals that still are the same or very similar to eir fossil selves are horseshoe crabs, nautilus, and even jellyfish![31]

ven things leaving the fossil record can tell scientists a lot of information out what happened in ancient waters and that can give them clues about w things in the ocean might change in the future. For example, a leontologist named Adriene Lam shared her research on plankton ssils.She's a researcher in a project that looks at the conditions of oceans ring periods of high temperatures in the past and she found out that ring some of the periods of warmer temperatures, the atmospheric nditions then are similar to how they are now.[32] So by looking at the ssils of past ocean life, scientists can make predictions about how changing nperatures and atmospheric conditions may change aquatic life on earth w.

3.3 CHECK YOUR KNOWLEDGE!

Check how much you remember from this chapter by answering the following questions!

1. *Why do most aquatic creatures live near the surface?*

2. *What happens to creatures that die in the water and sink to the bottom?*

3. *What are two common types of aquatic fossils you might find?*

4. *How old are trilobites and coral fossils?*

5. *Where can you find a wide variety of fish fossils, including stingrays and paddlefish?*

6. *What do scientists learn from studying how ancient animals evolved through the fossil record?*

7. *How can looking at past ocean life fossils help scientists make predictions about the future?*

Chapter 4:

❖

PLANT FOSSILS

PEERING INTO EARTH'S ANCIENT GREENERY

When learning about how animal fossils form in the first chapter, we covered that for fossils to form, the animals need to die and then their body needs to be covered quickly with layers of sediments or ash. The parts that do not decompose are the parts that later become fossils. This means that usually fossils are only created of the hard parts of animals – things like bones, scales, teeth, or claws. Softer things – like feathers – also fossilize but very rarely. So how to plant fossils form?

4.1 HOW PLANT FOSSILS FORM

Plant fossilization happens in much the same way as animal fossilization with one major difference. In order for the plant part to turn into a fossil, the plant needs to die and fall in an area that is anaerobic – th[...] means that an area has very low oxygen.[33] Why does the oxygen lev[...] matter? Well, in a normal environment, the oxygen in the atmosphere allow[...] for the plant to naturally decompose. Think about what happens if you pu[...] a leaf from a tree and drop it to the ground. Does it become a fossil? C[...] course not! In just a few months, that leaf will have completely disappeare[...] broken down by nature's own little garbage cleaners: invertebrates like bug[...] crabs, mushrooms, and even microbes.[34] So if the plant falls in an area whe[...] there is oxygen, these little garbage cleaners break down the plant parts in[...] tiny pieces that can then be recycled back into the environment.

a couple of leaf adpressions

But if the plant falls into an area that is anaerobic when it dies, th[...] garbage cleaners don't have a chance to break down any of the pla[...] parts. This happens most often when a leaf, flower, or stem falls into a ri[...] or lake. The plant part sinks down to the bottom of the water and then[...] covered by sediment.[33] These deep parts of lakes and rivers have no oxyg[...]

very few animals can live there. Then, like with marine fossilization, more
d more layers pile on and add pressure to the plant, creating the plant
ssil.

There are a few different types of plant fossils that can be found. The
ost common type of plant fossils are called depressions. These are formed
en the part of the plant has been compressed until it is flat. Then the
ape of the plant has been fully imprinted into the sediment. The sediment
rns into rock over thousands of years, creating the fossils.[35] If a plant has a
d or a stem that is really hard and tough, it could form a mold of the
int. This happens when the seed or plant part is buried in the sediment.
e sediment hardens around the seed, perfectly showing the shape and size
the seed or plant part. After the sediment hardens, the plant part decays,
ving the inside hollow.[33]

Petrified trees – trees that have been turned into rock – are a special
id of plant fossil that is formed in a slightly different way. Petrified trees
 made when the wood of the trunk and branches die and fall into
liment that is very wet. This wet sediment also must have a lot of dissolved
nerals in it when the dead tree falls into it. Because the tree has fallen into
iter, there is not enough oxygen for nature's garbage cleaners to
compose the tree. As the water flows through the wood of the tree, the cell
lls of the tree trunk are slowly replaced with the dissolved minerals.[36] Over
e, the tree completely turns to stone.

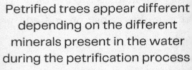
Petrified trees appear different depending on the different minerals present in the water during the petrification process

4.2 WHAT PLANT FOSSILS REVEAL

Like all of the other fossils in this book, there is a lot to be learne from plant fossils. Plants have a major impact on the planet; they produ oxygen for animals and they help to cool the temperature of earth as well. [38] Since they are so important to all creatures, scientists have been trying figure out when they first appeared but because plants don't have hard par like bones or teeth, they don't easily turn into fossils. Scientists have be trying to figure out when green plants first appeared on the fossil record with the assumption that marine plants appeared first – and then trying figure out when plants migrated to land.

In early 2020, an impressive discovery was made.Paleobotanists scientists who specialize in studying plant fossils – from Virginia Te University working in China found microfossils of green seaweed that were billion years old!Microfossils are very tiny fossils; these fossils are usually ily one or two cells big! Anyway, these microfossils give scientists a lot of ues about how plants evolved in the sea and then later on land. [37] This scovery changed the ages of plants in the fossil record. One of the scientists charge of the research said that the algae found is similar to a modern day een seaweed, both in shape and size. [37] This shows us that green seaweed is a vital part to both prehistoric and modern marine ecosystems.

The next big thing that plant fossils tell scientists about ancient osystems is when the plants started to grow on land. If paleontologists iow when specific species of land plants were growing and they also know ien specific herbivorous animals or dinosaurs were living, they can guess iat plants these animals or dinosaurs ate. So when did plants start to grow i dry land? Paleobotanists think that land plants evolved from freshwater kes or ponds.In times of very high temperatures or periods of no rain, the iter would dry up.

Modern
Liverwort

The algae in the water would need to evolve in ways that allowed them to survive these periods when the water was gone.[39] The earliest fossil evidence of land plants is from 470 million years ago. The fossil shows spores – a part of a plant or fungus that is used for reproduction [40] – from a type of plant called a liverwort.[39] Other types of plants evolved to live on dry land around the same time as liverworts are mosses and hornworts.   These plants are all low to the ground, making it easy to grow roots and transport water within the plant. The taller the plants became, the more difficult it was to move water throughout the plant. Plants like trees, flowers, and ferns didn't evolve until much later – not until about 70 million years later.   [41]

Plant fossils can tell us even more than just what dinosaurs ate in particular time period. They can actually help scientists today with their research on different energy sources and their research on climate change. Maybe you've heard the term 'fossil fuel?' Fossil fuel is another name for oil, natural gas, or coal [42] – all of which are used as energy sources in daily life! It is hard to imagine something like a dinosaur skeleton becoming the gas that powers your parents' car so let's take a moment to learn how prehistoric organisms became fuel for your home and school.

So, how exactly is fuel made from fossils? It all starts with the sun. Green plants grow by absorbing energy from the sun. They use a special process called 'photosynthesis.' Photosynthesis allows the plant cell to use energy from the sun to convert carbon dioxide and water into oxygen and glucose (which is a type of sugar). [43]

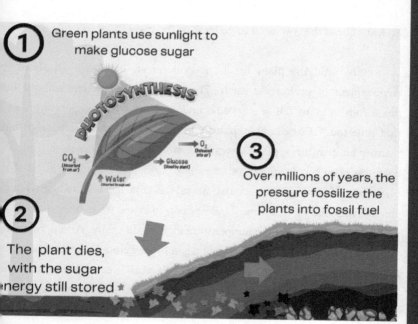

The oxygen is released into the atmosphere for the animals to use but e sugar is stored in the plant cells to be used as energy for the plant to ow.[42] When that green plant dies, it still contains all of the energy it stored the form of sugar. Pressure and time causes those plants to fossilize and ring the fossilization process, the sugar converts into different fuels. If the int that died is plankton, it forms natural gas or oil but if it was any other id of plant, it changes into coal.[42]

Humans have been using fossil fuels for over a thousand years with problems[44] but unfortunately, that is no longer the case. When fossil fuels used, they release carbon dioxide into the atmosphere. This carbon ixide traps heat in the atmosphere and this has been causing the iperature of the earth to steadily increase. [45]   While this is the first time it humans have made the temperature of the earth rise, it isn't the first ie in earth's history that the temperatures have changed so quickly. And to learn about that, we need to go back to the plant fossil record!

By studying plant fossils, paleobotanists can learn all about t environment of prehistoric earth. The plant fossils give clues about ho much rain or snow fell at a specific time and what the temperature was that time too.[46] For example, paleobotanists know that in places that ha warmer temperatures, plant leaves have smooth edges whereas if a place cold, the plant leaves are jagged or rough.[47] Scientists can look at all of t plant fossils found in one place that are all the same age and deduce what t climate was like at that time.[47] They can also see what happened to t plants in the past when the temperature increased rapidly. About 56 milli years ago, there was a period of time when there were a lot of natural ever happening that caused the temperature to increase very fast in a relative short time. The plant fossils from that time period shows that the ecosyster shifted as the temperatures changed around the world. Paleobotanists thir that this change in the fossil record shows them exactly what to expect modern-day temperatures continue to rise.[47]

4.3 CHECK YOUR KNOWLEDGE!

Check how much you remember from this chapter by answering the following questions.

What needs to happen for a plant part to turn into a fossil?

How do invertebrates like bugs, crabs, mushrooms, and microbes help break down plant parts?

What are adpressions, and how are they formed?

How are petrified trees formed differently from other plant fossils?

Why is it difficult for scientists to figure out when green plants first appeared on the fossil record?

What important discovery was made by paleobotanists from Virginia Tech University in China in early 2020?

How can plant fossils help scientists with research on energy sources and climate change?

Chapter 5:

———— ✤ ————

TRACE FOSSILS

FOLLOWING THE FOOTSTEPS OF ANCIENT LIFE

So far, almost all kinds of fossils have been discussed but there is one ore type out there that hasn't been talked about yet: trace fossils. These are fferent from all of the other types of fossils because these fossils aren't tually part of the living thing! They are just clues that the living thing left hind.

5.1 HOW TRACE FOSSILS FORM

Let's start by figuring out what exactly trace fossils are. All of the ssils that we have learned about in this book have been a type of fossil lled a 'body fossil.' This means that the fossil itself was formed with the imal or plant remains. [48]   On the other hand, a trace fossil is something left by the plants or animals. This includes things like eggs or eggshells, footprints, nests, or even poop! [48] Trace fossils are really important in the study of prehistoric plants and animals because they give scientists evidence on how the plant or animal moved, what they ate, or how they developed from baby to adult.[48]

Trace fossils are formed similarly to body fossils. Imagine this: a female dinosaur moves into an area with soft mud and makes a nest. Soon after that, she lays eggs in the nest. After some time, those eggs hatch, leaving behind eggshells. Eventually, all of the babies run around the nest, along with the mother. That family of dinosaurs then leaves the area. Afterwards, the soft mud hardens with the nest, footprints, and eggshells still there. Over time, these all get covered by sediment or volcanic ash. More and more layers cover the nest, footprints, and eggshells until the pressure from the layers compresses them and they turn into rock. This is generally how trace fossils are formed.

Footprints are an example of trace fossils

In the example about the mother, there are three different types of ace fossils mentioned: foot prints, eggshells, and a nest. But there are even ore things that can become trace fossils too! For example, you already arned that footprints can become trace fossils but did you know that other imal paths can become trace fossils too? For example, when an animal like worm burrows into soft mud and leaves a tunnel through the mud, those nnels can become trace fossils.[50] Many types of creepy crawlies made paths rough soft mud that later became trace fossils. [50]

There are two more types of trace fossils and both have to do with gestion. Gastroliths are found inside of an animal's intestine. They are all rocks that help the animal digest the food that they eat. A few modern- y animals still have them! Many birds that live on the ground, like triches or penguins have gastroliths and some other swimming animals like als or crocodiles have them. Several types of dinosaur fossils – mostly rbivores – were found with these stomach rocks in tact but it is also ssible to find them without other fossils. [51] The other digestion-related ce fossil is poop! Fossilized poop is called coprolites.[48] Dino poop can n into coprolites in two ways. One way is that after the dinosaur finishes business, the poop could have been covered quickly by sediments. This op breaks down after being buried so it leaves an imprint.[48] The other y is the poop petrifies – turns into stone in the same way that a tree does.[48]

5.2 WHAT TRACE FOSSILS REVEAL

So now that we know what trace fossils are and how they are formed, 's talk about why they are important. Ichnologists – the people who study ce fossils [52] – can learn a ton of information about how prehistoric animals ved and behaved before they died.

By studying paths of footprints, icnologists can learn a lot. They can learn:

- the size of a dinosaur
- the speed it was moving
- if it traveled alone or with a group

Look at this picture.

- Do you think this dinosaur traveled alone?
- Was this dinosaur running or walking slowly?

How did you figure out your answer?

For example, by studying dinosaur tracks, ichnologists have learned that some dinosaurs travel in large groups while others travel alone. [51] Researchers can also look at the tracks and see that dinosaurs that travel herds move in a way that keeps babies and young dinosaurs protected from possible predators. They can even tell that dinosaurs kept their tails held high by looking at the tracks; if dinosaurs let their tails touch the ground there would be tail marks between the footprints. [53]

Trace fossils of burrows tell scientists other things about prehistoric earth. By studying burrows in the fossil record, ichnologists can see when specific creatures evolved. For example, let's take a look at the earliest burrow in the fossil record. The oldest burrows are from 560 million years ago and these show that the creatures were only able to move horizontally across the ocean floor or just below the floor. They could not dig straight down.[52] Burrows dated from around 555 million years ago showed that atures had evolved to the point of being able to dig straight down.[52] ientists think that these early burrowers dug the burrows to find food and o to avoid getting eaten by predators.[52]

Speaking of predators, trace fossils also give clues about the ancient od web. One thing that wasn't mentioned earlier but is important to entists is that trace fossils do not have to only occur in wet mud. Bite rks are also considered trace fossils, specifically those on other fossilized nes. So paleontologists can look at bone fossils and if there are bite marks, y can tell that the animal was eaten by a predator.[54]

5.3 CHECK YOUR KNOWLEDGE!

Check how much you remember from this chapter by answering t
following questions.

1. *Trace fossils are formed from the remains of animals and plants.*

2. *Footprints, eggshells, and nests are examples of trace fossils.*

3. *Gastroliths are small rocks found inside an animal's stomach to help with digestion.*

4. *Ichnologists study trace fossils to learn about how prehistoric animals moved and behaved.*

5. *Bite marks on fossilized bones are not considered trace fossils.*

Chapter 6:

---❖---

FOSSIL HUNTING

CONNECTING TO THE PAST

y now, you're probably
ger to get out there and
y to find your own
ssils. Paleontologists
e still out in the fields,
gging up fossils and
arning from them…but
here in the world are
ey?

.1 FAMOUS FOSSIL
DIG LOCATIONS

hough fossils can be
und anywhere in the
orld, there are some
es that are very famous

r having lots of fossils that are easy to find. These are a few of the best dig
es for dinosaur fossils:

1.   HELL CREEK FORMATION, UNITED STATES

This fossil site is located across several US states (Montana, North
kota, South Dakota, and Wyoming). Many of the most famous
osaurs have been found here, including tyrannosaurus rexes and
eratops. Home to many more species than just dinosaurs, fossils of

mammals from the past have also been found here as well as prehistori
reptiles like alligators and turtles.[10]

2. RED BEDS, UNITED STATES

The Red Beds of Texas and Oklahoma in the US are home to fossil
of dinosaurs that have spines on their back, creating 'sails.'This include
dimetrodons and other four-legged animals similar to modern-day reptiles
The name 'Red Bed' refers to the type of rock layer that is found, so ther
are lots of other red bed fossil sites like this one throughout the sout
western part of the US. [10]

3. JIUFOTANG FORMATION, CHINA

China is a bit new to the paleontology world, becoming a popula
fossil location in recent years.The fossils at the Jiufotang Formation da
back to 120 million years ago and a very diverse group of fossils has bee
found here. Among the most notable are the feathered dinosaurs as well
prehistoric birds that have been found in this formation.[10]

4. EDIACARA HILLS, AUSTRALIA

This fossil site is known for being the place where multicellul:
(animals with more than one cell) life existed earlier than 540 million yea
ago. The name 'Ediacara' was given to this location because it was the fir
time a new time period had been named in over 100 years. At this site, t
first multicellular marine animal fossils were discovered. These include
animals like jellyfish, flatworms, and even the ancient ancestors to trilobites

5. LA BREA TAR PITS, UNITED STATES

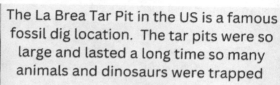
The La Brea Tar Pit in the US is a famous fossil dig location. The tar pits were so large and lasted a long time so many animals and dinosaurs were trapped

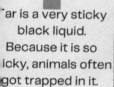
ar is a very sticky black liquid. Because it is so icky, animals often got trapped in it.

These tar pits are located inside the city of Los Angeles but they are ll regularly making new discoveries there! Scientists have been pulling sils out of the tar pits for over a hundred years, making this dig site redibly important. The interesting thing about this site is how the animals d. In the past, animals would get stuck in the sticky black tar. These imals then sank into the tar and died. Because the bodies didn't have the ance to decompose or get eaten after the animal died, the body was really ll-preserved, just like what happens with inclusions in amber. Things like er-toothed tigers and mammoths have been found in these tar pits. [10]

6.2 FINDING YOUR OWN FOSSILS

These sites all sound amazing! Now, it is important to remember that se sites are active dig sites for paleontologists so it is best to visit with a ined professional. If you live near these sites or your family is planning a

trip near these places, it is often possible to book tours to active dig site
Then you can see how scientists work.

Going with a tour group gives you the chance to watch real scientists making discoveries!

But that is not to say that you can't find your own fossils too! Findi
fossils is actually a bit simpler than it seems. Of course, if you want to fi
your own fossils, you'll need to know where to start. So, how
paleontologists find fossils? To find fossils, paleontologists study the di
Well, not really the dirt itself, but the dirt layers. As sediment settles ov
time, they form layers underground which – after many years and a lot
pressure – turn into rock. These rock layers are called strata. The field
science where these layers are studied is called stratigraphy and it is one
the sciences that paleontologists use to figure out where different kinds
fossils are.[9] Paleontologists know how old each layer of strata is and th
also know how old the fossils are that they are looking for. They can use t
information to know how deeply to dig at a fossil site.

These layers of rock are called strata. If you see an area where many layers are exposed, there's a chance you can find your own fossils here!

So, in order for you to find your own fossils and start building your fossil collection, you need to know where to look. As was mentioned earlier, fossils are stuck in layers of sediment so the best place to start looking is in places where you can see multiple layers of sediment, multiple strata, at the same time. The best place to see this is called a 'rock outcrop.' Outcrops are places where wind, water, or creatures have worn away the outer layers of dirt and now the sediment layers are visible.[11]

It is also possible to find fossils along coastlines. This is actually one of the most common ways to find amber. If you want to find amber, it is best to wait until after a big storm. The storm often frees the amber from the seabed, after which it is washed up onto the beach. You'll need to go when the water is at low tide. Beaches in Europe are where you will have the most luck finding amber – especially around the Baltic Sea.[12]

Walking along the coastline is also a good way to find fossils that aren't amber. Jurassic Coast in England is famous for the 95 miles of fossil-rich coastline. Here, the cliffs have 185 million years of Earth's history exposed to the wind and rain. This means that there are fossils being uncovered daily. Because of this, it is the most popular place to hunt for fossils in all of the UK. You can find all sorts of fossils here, but the most common ones are ammonites and prehistoric fish.[10] If you want to try to find fossils along a coastline, make sure you look for coasts where multiple layers of strata are visible. Much like an outcrop, these areas will be affected by wind, water, and other creatures and that means you will have better luck finding hidden treasures!

Jurassic Coast in the UK is a well–known spot for fossil hunting. There are 95 miles of coastline where marine fossils are common.

Now that you know where to go to find your fossils, the next step is to be very patient and very observant. Fossils are difficult to find and there is a lot of sediment to look at. Patience is really the key to finding fossils.

6.3 SAFE AND LEGAL FOSSIL HUNTING

Fossil hunting is a fun hobby that is a bit like treasure hunting. Treasure hunting is mostly connected with pirates on the open sea. Unfort-

nately, pirates aren't known for being safe or being good at following the
w. So while we want to find lots of fossil treasures, we also want to make
re that we are doing it in a safe and legal way. So, what are the rules for
ssil hunting?

- Ask an adult to check that it is legal to dig for and keep fossils in
  your area.
  - This can be a challenge as many US states and even different
    countries have different laws about this.[12]
  - If you are not sure, ask a park ranger or information desk in the
    park where you plan to fossil hunt.
- Only enter areas that you have permission to enter.
  - If you aren't sure, ask an adult.
- Always go fossil hunting with an adult
- Be sure to plan where you will be going to hunt fossils and share this
  plan with an adult that is not going with you.
- Pack properly for the day:
  - A magnifying glass
  - Lots and lots of water
  - Some toilet paper or paper towels to wrap the fossils you find
  - Soft brushes to brush dirt away from fossils

  Old toothbrushes can be used for this!

6.4 IDENTIFYING YOUR DISCOVERIES

The final part of your fossil hunting journey is to document and
ntify your findings. It is important that you document what fossils you
d in your journal, along with the date and location. These records can
p you find patterns in the fossil types you are finding in specific locations.

Let's start with identifying your amber finds. How can you tell if you
nd regular old resin or amazing amber? To identify amber, just trust your
se! This is actually the simplest method to test if the amber you found is
lly amber.Real amber smells like pine trees when heated up. So to test
ur amber, take it in your hands and rub your hands together fast while

holding the amber to warm up it us. Then, hold it to your nose and take
deep breath. If you smell pine trees, then you've found a genuine piece c
amber!Another way you can test amber is to put it in a cup of salt wate
from the sea or ocean. Amber is lighter than sea water, so it should float i
the cup.[13]

To identify your other fossils, we can separate them into fou
categories: invertebrate, vertebrate, plant, and trace. The following section
include the most common things you can find in each category.

Invertebrate Fossils:

Brachiopods

crinoid

ammonite

Brachiopods and ammonite
are very common invertebrat
fossils. Crinoids are also callec
'sea lilies' and are often founc
in areas with other marin
fossils.The 'stem' part of the

inoid is what is most commonly found.

is also likely that you will find corals in these areas with high marine fossil posits. There are both solitary coral fossils and colony coral fossils. olitary coral fossils look a bit like a claw or a horn while colony coral fossils ok like a repeated pattern in the rock.

ertebrate Fossils:

teeth

The most common mammal fossil that you are likely to find are the th of some prehistoric animal. In some areas of the world, it is also easy to d fossilized fish too.

Fish
The most common type of fish fossil found is the Knightia fish

Plant Fossils:

Ferns

If you are lucky enough to find a plant fossil, there's a good chance will be of a kind of fern.

race Fossils:

ootprints

If you're very very lucky, you might even find footprints! Of the fferent kinds of trace fossils, footprints are the most easily recognizable as ssils.

Another important step to fossil hunting is documenting where you und which fossils. Whether you find something amazing or nothing at all, ite it down! This will allow you to know where to go next time. To help u keep track of the places you've searched and your findings, it is a good ea to carry a small notebook with you to write stuff down.[11] When you're iting stuff in your notebook, make sure you include the date, where you nt, who you went with, and what you found. It is nice to include both a itten description and a sketch or drawing of your fossil finds. These things easy to forget so it is very important to write them down on the same y! Imagine you find a great fossil one day and a year later you want to do ne more fossil hunting in the same spot. If you don't write down all the ails in your journal, you may miss out on more great fossils in the future. u can see an example of a fossil hunting notebook page on the next page.

Date: December 5, 2021
Place: Devonian Fossil Gorge, Coralville Lake, Iowa
Who: Dad, Gwen, Olive, Chris, and Rhya

What was found:

There were so many marine fossils here. We found brachipods colony corals and solitary corals, and crinoid stems. Everything we found was stuck to larger rocks so we were not able to tak any of the fossils home.

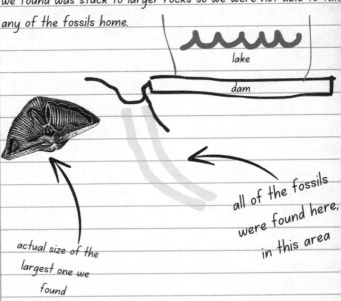

lake

dam

all of the fossils were found here, in this area

actual size of the largest one we found

6.5 CHECK YOUR KNOWLEDGE!

Check how much you remember from this chapter by reading the following sentences. Some of the sentences are true and some are false. How can you make the false sentences true?

The Hell Creek Formation is only located in Montana.

The Red Beds are named because of the color of the rock layers found here.

The Jiufotang Formation in China is known for fossils of feathered dinosaurs.

The La Brea Tar Pits are located in New York City.

It is best to look for fossils along coastlines after a big storm.

Conclusion:

❖

UNCOVERING EARTH'S TIMELESS TREASURES

As we come to the end of our journey through Earth's ancient past, I hope you've discovered just how fascinating fossils can be. These incredible relics of the past are more than just old rocks—they are stories set in stone, waiting for someone like you to unlock their secrets.

We've learned that fossils are made in different ways, depending on where and how an ancient creature or plant died. Whether it's a mighty dinosaur being buried in layers of mud and dirt, a tiny insect trapped in amber, or a sea creature fossilized in ocean sediments, each fossil is a special and valuable piece of Earth's history. Through these fossils, we can see how life on Earth has changed over millions of years.

Fossils are like clues in a giant puzzle, helping us understand what life was like in the distant past. They tell us about creatures that no longer exist, show us how continents have shifted, and even give us insights into ancient climates. With each fossil, we get a little closer to understanding the grand story of life on Earth. With each fossil, we learn more about how the past can tell us about our planet's present and future.

And now, armed with all this knowledge, you might be eager to find your own fossils. Remember, fossil hunting is like a treasure hunt, but it's important to do it safely and legally. Always make sure you have permission to search in the areas you choose, and never take fossils from protected sites like national parks or private land without proper authorization. Check local laws in your area as these are different all over the world. Fossils are precious, and we need to protect them for future generations to study and

enjoy.

As you continue you adventure into the world o fossils, I hope you carry wit you the excitement an curiosity that brought you this book in the first plac There are so many mo discoveries to be made, an who knows? Maybe one da you'll uncover a fossil that te a brand-new chapter in Eart story.

Thank you for reading until t end. I hope you enjoyed this journey through time as much as I enjoyed guiding you through it. If yo found this book helpful or educational, I would love to hear your thought Please consider leaving a review on Amazon to help other young explore like you discover the wonders of fossils. You can find the review link in t QR codes on the next page.

Happy fossil hunting, and may your adventures be filled with discovery!

Thank you again for reading my book. As an independent author that is
st starting out, it would mean so much to me if you could leave an honest
review. You can find the link to my author profile (which includes this
book) below:

And if you liked this book, you can check out my other titles using
the link above too.

In-Text References

---❖---

Page2. (n.d.). http://www.fossilsforkids.com/Page2.html

How do fossils form? (n.d.). The Australian Museum. https://australian.museum/learn/australia-over-time/fossils/how-do-fossils-form/

Why do some things become fossils, but others do not? (2016, December 9). American Geosciences Institute. https://www.americangeosciences.org/education/k5geosource/activities/investigations/fossils/how-fossils-form

Beyond Jurassic World: what we really know about dinosaurs and how. (2018, June 25). Natural History Museum. https://www.nhm.ac.uk/discover/what-can-scientists-learn-about-dinosaurs-and-how.html

Biology:Dinosaur behavior - HandWiki. (n.d.). https://handwiki.org/wiki/Biology:Dinosaur_behavior

Why are birds the only surviving dinosaurs? (2018, May 23). [Video]. Natural History Museum. https://www.nhm.ac.uk/discover/why-are-birds-the-only-surviving-dinosaurs.html

Wikipedia contributors. (2003, August 20). Theropoda. Wikipedia. https://en.wikipedia.org/wiki/Theropoda

PALEONTOLOGY: THE WINDOW TO SCIENCE EDUCATION. (n.d.). https://ucmp.berkeley.edu/fosrec/Stucky.html

In the Field: Following the Work of a Paleontologist. (n.d.). https://carnegiemnh.org/in-the-field-following-the-work-of-a-paleontologist/

).Charles. (2017, June 15). 10 of the Best Fossil Sites in the World - Earthly Universe. Earthly Universe. https://earthlyuniverse.com/10-best-fossil-sites-world/

.Finding Fossils | AMNH. (n.d.). American Museum of Natural History. https://www.amnh.org/explore/ology/paleontology/finding-fossils2

12. How to find prehistoric amber. (2019, March 2). Sciencing. https://sciencing.com/prehistoric-amber-7516630.html

13. Robert and Victoria - Jet Manufacturers Est. 1979. (n.d.-b). 8 ways to identify genuine Baltic amber. https://rvwhitbyjet.co.uk/blogs/news/8-ways-to-identify-genuine-baltic-amber?srsltid=AfmBOoqzJQ9H2IRtEiX26oh1Jya27c04XQnye8t-SHi2Lx47Hb1x_63P

14. Greshko, M. (2023, April 6). How amber creates exquisite fossils. Science. https://www.nationalgeographic.com/science/article/what-is-amber-fossils-science

15. Wikipedia contributors. (2024, August 16). Arthropod. Wikipedia. https://en.wikipedia.org/wiki/Arthropod

16. Mheslinga. (2023, August 30). Carbon-14 dating, explained. University of Chicago News. https://news.uchicago.edu/explainer/what-is-carbon-14-dating

17. http://treeplantation.com. (n.d.). Insights into the Jurassic period. Tree Plantation. https://treeplantation.com/amber-insects.html

18. Trapped in time: The top 10 amber fossils. (n.d.). Earth Archives. https://eartharchives.org/articles/trapped-in-time-the-top-10-amber-fossils/index.html

19. Birks, H. (2008). Paleoecology. In Elsevier eBooks (pp. 2623–2634). https://doi.org/10.1016/b978-008045405-4.00525-5

20. Discovery in amber reveals ancient biology of termites. (2017, October 5). Life at OSU. https://today.oregonstate.edu/archives/2009/may/discovery-amber-reveals-ancient-biology-termites

21. Wikipedia contributors. (2024b, August 17). Amber - Wikipedia. https://en.wikipedia.org/wiki/Amber

22. Under what conditions do fossils form? (2016, November 17). America Geosciences Institute.

https://www.americangeosciences.org/education/k5geosource/content/fossils/under-what-conditions-do-fossils-form

3. Collecting guide to fossil fish 11641. (2023, April 23). Christie's. https://www.christies.com/en/stories/collecting-guide-to-fossil-fish-f7a4a9e4f96a4b0b9a399935a328b1ee

4. limestone | AMNH. (n.d.). American Museum of Natural History. https://www.amnh.org/explore/ology/ology-cards/245-limestone

5. Geologic time. (n.d.). https://ucmp.berkeley.edu/education/explorations/tours/geotime/gtpage7.html

6. The Editors of Encyclopaedia Britannica. (2024, July 14). Trilobite | Cambrian period, Extinction, Arthropod, & Facts. Encyclopedia Britannica. https://www.britannica.com/animal/trilobite

7. British Geological Survey. (2021, August 20). Corals - British Geological Survey. https://www.bgs.ac.uk/discovering-geology/fossils-and-geological-time/corals/

8. Doran, A., & Doran, A. (2022, December 5). Fossilized Colonial Coral Identification Guide. Sisyphos Rocks. https://sisyphos.rocks/fossilized-colonial-coral-identification-guide/#mobile-menu

9. Fossil Fish - Fossil Butte National Monument (U.S. National Park Service). (n.d.). https://www.nps.gov/fobu/learn/nature/fossil-fish.htm

10. What were trilobites? (n.d.). Oxford University Museum of Natural History. https://oumnh.ox.ac.uk/learn-what-were-trilobites

11. Brauner, E. (2022, December 12). These Prehistoric Ocean Animals are Still Around Today. Ocean Conservancy. https://oceanconservancy.org/blog/2019/02/13/prehistoric-ocean-animals-still-around-today/

12. What tiny fossils can tell us about the changing climate - Binghamton News. (n.d.). News - Binghamton University. https://www.binghamton.edu/news/story/4494/research-currents-what-tiny-fossils-can-tell-us-about-the-changing-climate

33. Lab III - Preservation (2). (n.d.).
https://ucmp.berkeley.edu/IB181/VPL/Pres/Pres2.html

34. Poppick, L. (2020). The life that springs from dead leaves in streams.
Knowable Magazine. https://doi.org/10.1146/knowable-080620-1

35. Wikipedia contributors. (2024a, August 7). Paleobotany. Wikipedia.
https://en.wikipedia.org/wiki/Paleobotany

36. Wikipedia contributors. (2024d, August 30). Petrified wood. Wikipedia
https://en.wikipedia.org/wiki/Petrified_wood

37. 1 billion-year-old green seaweed fossils identified, relative of modern
land plants. (2020, February 24). EurekAlert!
https://www.eurekalert.org/news-releases/900037

38. Pennisi, E. (2018, February 19). Land plants arose earlier than thought
—and may have had a bigger impact on the evolution of animals.
Science.org. Retrieved August 31, 2024, from
https://www.science.org/content/article/land-plants-arose-earlier-
thought-and-may-have-had-bigger-impact-evolution-animals

39. Great Moments in Plant Evolution, Part 1: Plants Invade the Land -
Brooklyn Botanic Garden. (n.d.). Brooklyn Botanic Garden.
https://www.bbg.org/article/great_moments_in_plant_evolution_plants
nvade_the_land

40. The Editors of Encyclopaedia Britannica. (1998, July 20). Spore |
Definition, Types, & Examples. Encyclopedia Britannica.
https://www.britannica.com/science/spore-biology

41. Bolkin, K. (2021, June 27). A brief history of Trees - TreesCharlotte.
TreesCharlotte. https://treescharlotte.org/tree-education/a-brief-history
of-trees/

42. What are fossil fuels? (2023, October 25). Smithsonian Ocean.
https://ocean.si.edu/conservation/gulf-oil-spill/what-are-fossil-fuels

43. Photosynthesis. (n.d.).
https://education.nationalgeographic.org/resource/photosynthesis/

44. Fossil Energy Study Guide: Coal. (n.d.). Department of Energy.
https://www.energy.gov/sites/prod/files/Elem_Coal_Studyguide.pdf

5. Fossil fuels and climate change: the facts. (2024, April 19). ClientEarth. https://www.clientearth.org/latest/news/fossil-fuels-and-climate-change-the-facts/

6. Banerjee, N. (2023, March 28). Plant Fossils: A peek into Earth's Past - Wildlife SOS. Wildlife SOS. https://wildlifesos.org/chronological-news/plant-fossils-a-peek-into-earths-past/

7. Magazine, S. (2021, April 28). What fossil plants reveal about climate change. Smithsonian Magazine. https://www.smithsonianmag.com/blogs/national-museum-of-natural-history/2021/04/29/what-fossil-plants-reveal-about-climate-change/

8. Amendolare, N. (n.d.). Trace Fossil | Definition, Types & Examples. Study.com. Retrieved September 1, 2024, from https://study.com/academy/lesson/trace-fossil-definition-lesson.html

9. How does a footprint become a fossil? (2016, December 9). American Geosciences Institute. https://www.americangeosciences.org/education/k5geosource/activities/investigations/fossils/fossil-footprints

10. Trace fossils. (n.d.). WGNHS. https://home.wgnhs.wisc.edu/wisconsin-geology/fossils/trace-fossils/

11. Gastroliths. (n.d.). https://ucmp.berkeley.edu/taxa/verts/archosaurs/gastroliths.php

12. Wikipedia contributors. (2024a, August 5). Trace fossil - Wikipedia. https://en.wikipedia.org/wiki/Trace_fossil

13. What can fossil footprints tell us? (2016, December 9). American Geosciences Institute. https://www.americangeosciences.org/education/k5geosource/activities/investigations/fossils/what-can-fossil-footprints-tell-us

14. Importance Of Trace Fossils In Paleontology. (n.d.). Faster Capital. Retrieved September 1, 2024, from https://fastercapital.com/topics/importance-of-trace-fossils-in-paleontology.html

Check Your Knowledge!

❖

Answers

Chapter 1 Check Your Knowledge Answers: 1. C 2. B 3. B 4. A 5. B

Chapter 2 Check Your Knowledge Answers: 1. C 2. D 3. D 4. C 5. D

Chapter 3 Check Your Knowledge Answers:

1. The water near the surface of lakes, rivers, and oceans is oxygen-ric because there is a lot of oxygen available for the animals.

2. Creatures that die in the water and sink to the bottom eventually get crushed under immense pressure and turn into limestone.

3. Two common types of aquatic fossils you might find are ammonites an brachiopods.

4. Trilobites are over 521 million years old, while coral has been around since around 500 million years ago.

5. In Fossil Butte, Wyoming (USA), you can find a wide variety of fish fossils, including stingrays and paddlefish.

6. Scientists learn about how ancient animals evolved by studying change in the fossil record over time.

7. Looking at past ocean life fossils helps scientists make predictions abou how changing temperatures and atmospheric conditions may affect aquati life on earth now.

Chapter 4 Check Your Knowledge Answers:

. The plant needs to die and fall in an area that is anaerobic.

. Invertebrates like bugs, crabs, mushrooms, and microbes break down plant parts into tiny pieces.

. Adpressions are formed when the part of the plant has been compressed until it is flat and imprinted into sediment.

. Petrified trees are formed when the wood of the trunk and branches falls into wet sediment with dissolved minerals, slowly turning into stone.

. Plants don't easily turn into fossils because they don't have hard parts like bones or teeth.

. Paleobotanists found microfossils of green seaweed that were 1 billion years old in China.

. Plant fossils can help scientists with research on energy sources like fossil fuels and climate change.

Chapter 5 Check Your Knowledge Answers:

False - Trace fossils are something left by the plants or animals, not formed from their remains.

True - Footprints, eggshells, and nests are mentioned as examples of trace fossils.

True - Gastroliths are described as small rocks that help animals digest food.

True - Ichnologists study trace fossils to learn about the movement and behavior of prehistoric animals.

False - Bite marks on fossilized bones are considered trace fossils.

Chapter 6 Check Your Knowledge Answers:

1. False - The Hell Creek Formation is located in several US states, not just Montana.

2. True - The Red Beds are named because of the type of rock layer found there, which is red.

3. True - The Jiufotang Formation is known for fossils of feathered dinosaurs.

4. False - The La Brea Tar Pits are located in Los Angeles, not New York City.

5. True - It is best to look for fossils along coastlines after a big storm.

Made in the USA
Las Vegas, NV
13 December 2024

14205074R00046